WNBA Hot Ticket

LAS VEGAS ACES

JOSH ANDERSON

Lerner Publications ◆ Minneapolis

To Leo and Dane, the biggest superstars I've ever met.

The stats and information in this book are accurate through the 2024 WNBA season.

Copyright © 2026 by Lerner Publishing Group, Inc.

All rights reserved. International copyright secured. No part of this book may be reproduced, stored in a retrieval system, or transmitted in any form or by any means—electronic, mechanical, photocopying, recording, or otherwise—without the prior written permission of Lerner Publishing Group, Inc., except for the inclusion of brief quotations in an acknowledged review.

Lerner Publications Company
An imprint of Lerner Publishing Group, Inc.
241 First Avenue North
Minneapolis, MN 55401 USA

For reading levels and more information, look up this title at www.lernerbooks.com.

Main body text set in Aptifer Slab LT Pro / Typeface provided by Linotype AG

Library of Congress Cataloging-in-Publication Data

Names: Anderson, Josh, author.
Title: Las Vegas Aces / Josh Anderson.
Description: Minneapolis : Lerner Publications, 2026 | Series: WNBA hot ticket (Lerner sports) | Includes bibliographical references and index. | Audience: Ages 7–11 | Audience: Grades 2–3 | Summary: "The Las Vegas Aces won back-to-back WNBA championships in 2022 and 2023. They were the first repeat champions in more than 20 years. Discover how the Aces made it to the top of the WNBA"—Provided by publisher.
Identifiers: LCCN 2024046185 (print) | LCCN 2024046186 (ebook) | ISBN 9798765670071 (library binding) | ISBN 9798765683545 (paperback) | ISBN 9798765682012 (epub)
Subjects: LCSH: Las Vegas Aces (Basketball team)—Juvenile literature. | Women's National Basketball Association—Juvenile literature.
Classification: LCC GV885.52.L37 A534 2026 (print) | LCC GV885.52.L37 (ebook) | DDC 796.32309793/13—dc23/eng/20241231

LC record available at https://lccn.loc.gov/2024046185
LC ebook record available at https://lccn.loc.gov/2024046186

Manufactured in the United States of America
1 – CG – 12/15/24

TABLE OF CONTENTS

A PERFECT POSTSEASON 4

FACTS AT A GLANCE 5

CHAPTER 1
A TEAM ON THE MOVE 9

CHAPTER 2
AMAZING STARS 15

CHAPTER 3
FIRST CHAMPIONSHIP 23

CHAPTER 4
A DYNASTY IN THE MAKING 27

Glossary................................. 30
Learn More 31
Index 32

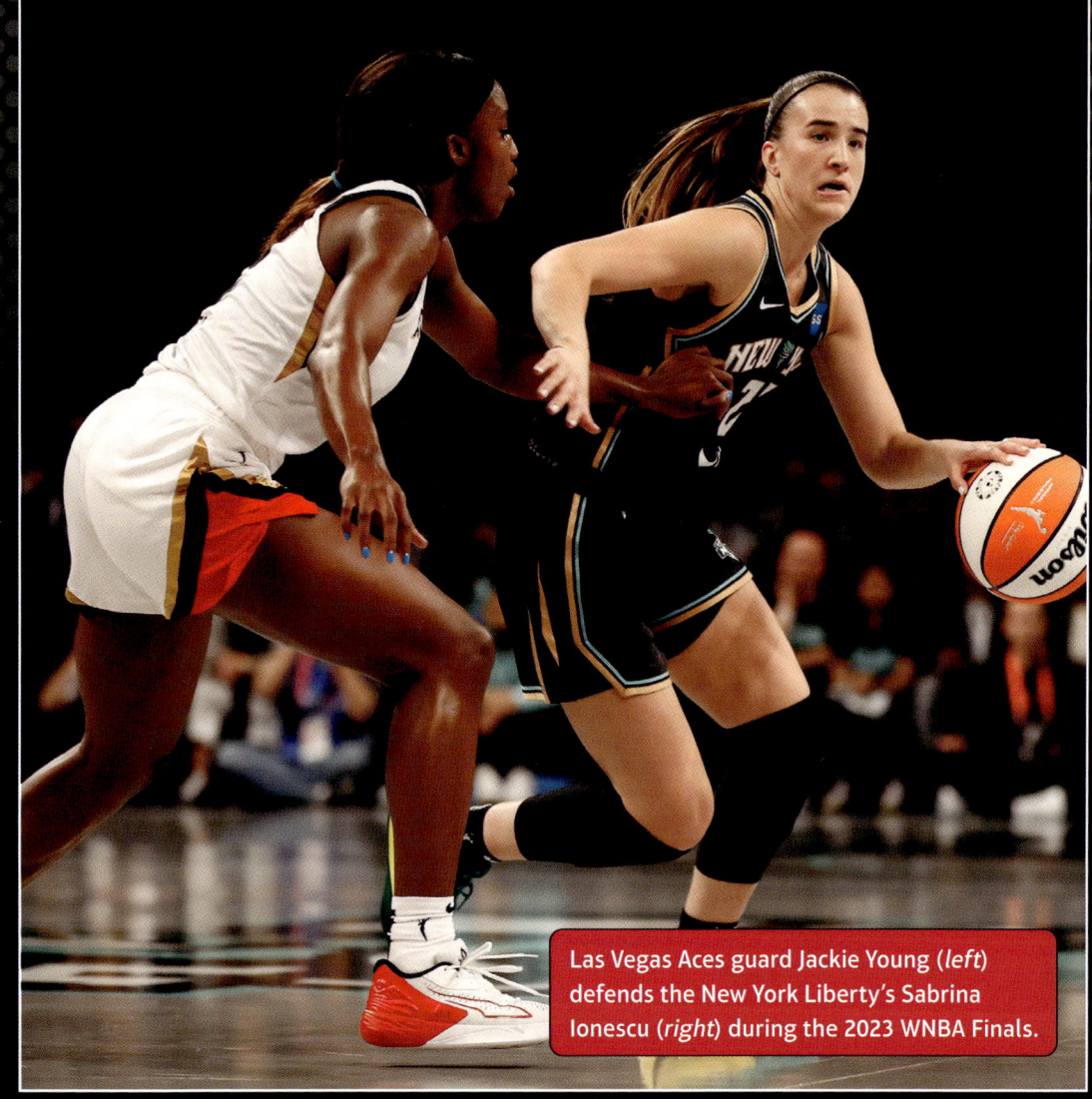

Las Vegas Aces guard Jackie Young (*left*) defends the New York Liberty's Sabrina Ionescu (*right*) during the 2023 WNBA Finals.

A PERFECT POSTSEASON

FACTS AT A GLANCE

- In 2023, the **LAS VEGAS ACES** became the first Women's National Basketball Association (WNBA) team in 21 years to win back-to-back championships.
- In 1998, the team drafted the tallest player in WNBA history, 7-foot-2 (2.2 m) **MARGO DYDEK**.
- **A'JA WILSON** has won the WNBA's Most Valuable Player (MVP) award three times, in 2020, 2022, and 2024.
- A'ja Wilson tied the WNBA single-game scoring record in 2023 with **53 POINTS**.

New York Liberty guard Sabrina Ionescu stood on the sideline, looking for a teammate to receive a pass. Las Vegas Aces defenders guarded Ionescu's teammates. The Aces hoped to leave no player open. One stop was all they needed.

There were 8.8 seconds left in Game 4 of the 2023 WNBA Finals. Holding a 70–69 lead, the Aces hoped to prevent New York from scoring. If they could, they'd become the first WNBA team to win back-to-back championships in 21 years.

It took several seconds for Ionescu to find a target. She tossed the ball to New York's star, Breanna Stewart, who was guarded by Aces forward Alysha Clark. Clark had been part of the WNBA's All-Defensive Team twice. Stewart tried to dribble around Clark. Aces guard Jackie Young joined Clark to help stop Stewart.

Betnijah Laney-Hamilton, the Liberty player Young had been guarding, was open behind the three-point line. Stewart passed to Laney-Hamilton. But before Laney-Hamilton could shoot, Aces guard Kelsey Plum moved over to stop her. With less than three seconds left, Laney-Hamilton threw a desperate pass to Liberty teammate Courtney Vandersloot in the corner.

Vandersloot had to shoot quickly, and Young tried to stop her. Young jumped into the air with her arm up. Vandersloot's wild shot didn't go anywhere near the basket. The ball landed in another player's hands as the game clock reached zero. In the final moments, the Aces had played the same incredible defense that led them to a title in 2022 and a record 34 wins in 2023. They were champions once again.

Aces players, coaches, and team officials celebrate their second WNBA championship in a row in 2023.

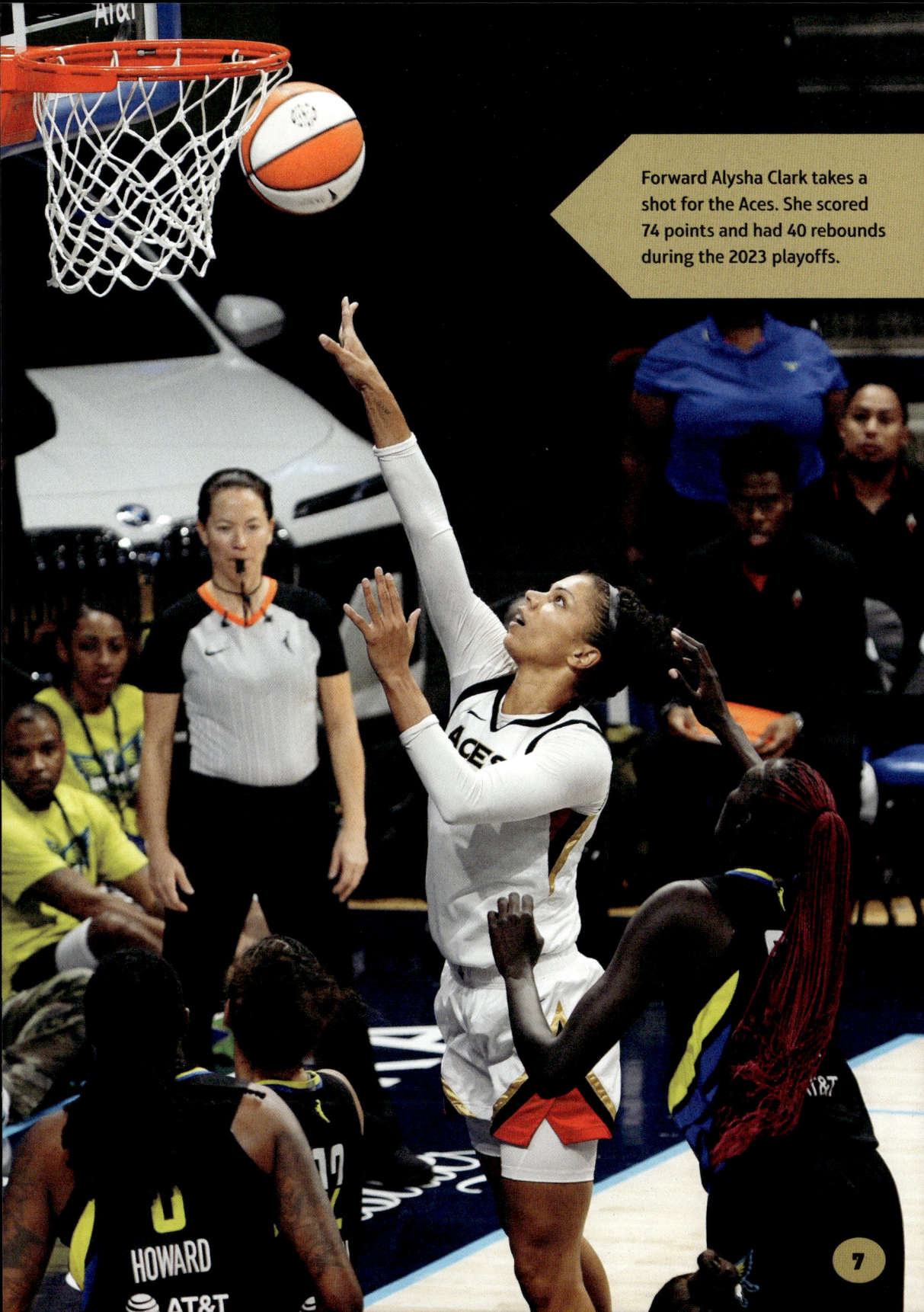

Forward Alysha Clark takes a shot for the Aces. She scored 74 points and had 40 rebounds during the 2023 playoffs.

Guard Marie Ferdinand-Harris shoots a free throw for the Utah Starzz during a 2001 game.

CHAPTER 1
A TEAM ON THE MOVE

The Aces are one of the eight original teams from the WNBA's first season in 1997. Back then, the team was called the Utah Starzz. The double Z in *Starzz* was used to match the state's National Basketball Association (NBA) team, the Utah Jazz. The Starzz played their first six seasons in Utah.

Margo Dydek (*center right*) and her teammates talk about their next move during a time-out in a 2000 game against the Seattle Storm.

After finishing with the league's worst record in 1997, the Starzz picked first in the 1998 WNBA Draft. They selected 7-foot-2 (2.2 m) Margo Dydek. Dydek played seven seasons for the team and is the tallest player ever to play in the WNBA. The team's last three seasons in Utah included more wins than losses. The Starzz made the playoffs for the first time in 2001. They made it again in 2002.

After the 2002 season, the Starzz were sold to the owner of the NBA's San Antonio Spurs. The new owner moved the team to San Antonio, Texas. Playing as the Silver Stars, the team's first four seasons were not successful.

Although she was known for her blocking skills, Margo Dydek scored 2,457 points during her seven seasons with the team.

In her 26 WNBA playoff games with the Stars, Becky Hammon averaged 18.2 points per game.

A trade before the 2007 season brought All-Star Becky Hammon to San Antonio. Hammon teamed up with young forward Sophia Young-Malcolm to lead San Antonio to six straight playoff appearances from 2007 to 2012. They made it to the WNBA Finals in 2008. The Silver Stars lost in three games to the Detroit Shock (now the Dallas Wings).

In 2014, the team dropped *Silver* from their name and played the next four seasons as the San Antonio Stars. Before the 2018 season, the team was again on the move—this time to Las Vegas, Nevada. In their new home, the team became the Las Vegas Aces. They made their Vegas home at an arena inside the Mandalay Bay Hotel.

HOOPS SCOOP

In 2020, A'ja Wilson became the first WNBA MVP in team history.

A'ja Wilson (*right*) takes a shot over the outstretched arm of the Seattle Storm's Breanna Stewart (*left*) in 2018.

Before their first season in Las Vegas, the Aces drafted center A'ja Wilson first overall in the WNBA Draft. Wilson soon became one of the top stars in the game, winning the league's Rookie of the Year award in 2018. She has also been named the WNBA's MVP three times. The Aces' time in Las Vegas has been the team's greatest period of success so far. The Aces have played in the WNBA Finals three times since moving to Las Vegas and have won two WNBA championships.

MAKING THE NEWS

In 2020, many people in the US protested the treatment of Black Americans by police officers. Many protesters also wanted to make sure that LGBTQIA+ citizens could live peacefully and have equal rights. One way the Aces brought attention to these matters was to include reminders and quotes about them in their game notes. Game notes are given to writers and league officials before and after WNBA games. The notes encouraged writers to pay more attention to the protests. The team continues the practice to remind people of important issues in the United States.

Game notes allow the Aces to speak to their fans through the reporters who cover the games on TV.

Stars forward Sophia Young-Malcolm (*right*) tries to score against the Phoenix Mercury. Young-Malcolm played her entire WNBA career with the team.

CHAPTER 2
AMAZING STARS

Because of her incredible height, center Margo Dydek was the team's best-known player during many of its early seasons. Dydek joined the Starzz in 1998 and played with the team for seven seasons. She was at her best on the defensive end of the floor. Dydek was the best shot blocker in the history of the WNBA. She holds the league's all-time record with 877 blocks in her career.

Margo Dydek (*right*) blocks a shot from Cynthia Cooper of the Houston Comets during a 1998 game.

During her nine seasons with the Silver Stars, Sophia Young-Malcolm (*center*) scored 14.3 points and grabbed six rebounds per game.

San Antonio drafted forward Sophia Young-Malcolm in 2006. Young-Malcolm made an immediate impact. She averaged 12 points and 7.6 rebounds per game as a rookie and helped the team almost double their win total. After her first season, she helped lead the Silver Stars to six straight playoff appearances. Young-Malcolm played her entire nine-season career for San Antonio and was a three-time All-Star.

In 2007, a year after drafting Young-Malcolm, the team traded for New York Liberty guard Becky Hammon. Already one of the best guards in the WNBA, Hammon upped her game even more after coming to San Antonio. She averaged 15.6 points per game with the Stars, more than five points per game better than she had averaged in New York. She also increased her assist average from 2.5 to 5.1 per game.

Hammon helped lead San Antonio to the playoffs in seven of her eight seasons with the team. Her 1,708 assists rank sixth all-time in the WNBA. Hammon is also a member of the Basketball Hall of Fame.

Becky Hammon (*right*) dribbles around Indiana Fever defender Sydney Carter during a 2014 game.

After her retirement as a player in 2014, Hammon began an incredible coaching career. She became the first full-time female coach in NBA history when she joined the San Antonio Spurs. Then she became the first woman to serve as a head coach in the NBA's Summer League. She was hired to coach her old team, the Aces, before the 2022 season. Her time coaching the team has been a great success. The Aces won the WNBA title in each of her first two seasons.

Becky Hammon spent eight seasons as an assistant coach with the San Antonio Spurs before becoming head coach of the Aces.

In 2024, A'ja Wilson became the first player in WNBA history to score 1,000 points in a single season.

The biggest Aces superstar is center A'ja Wilson. Since entering the league in 2018, Wilson has put together a Hall of Fame-worthy career. Averaging 20.7 points and eight rebounds in her first year, she won the WNBA's Rookie of the Year award.

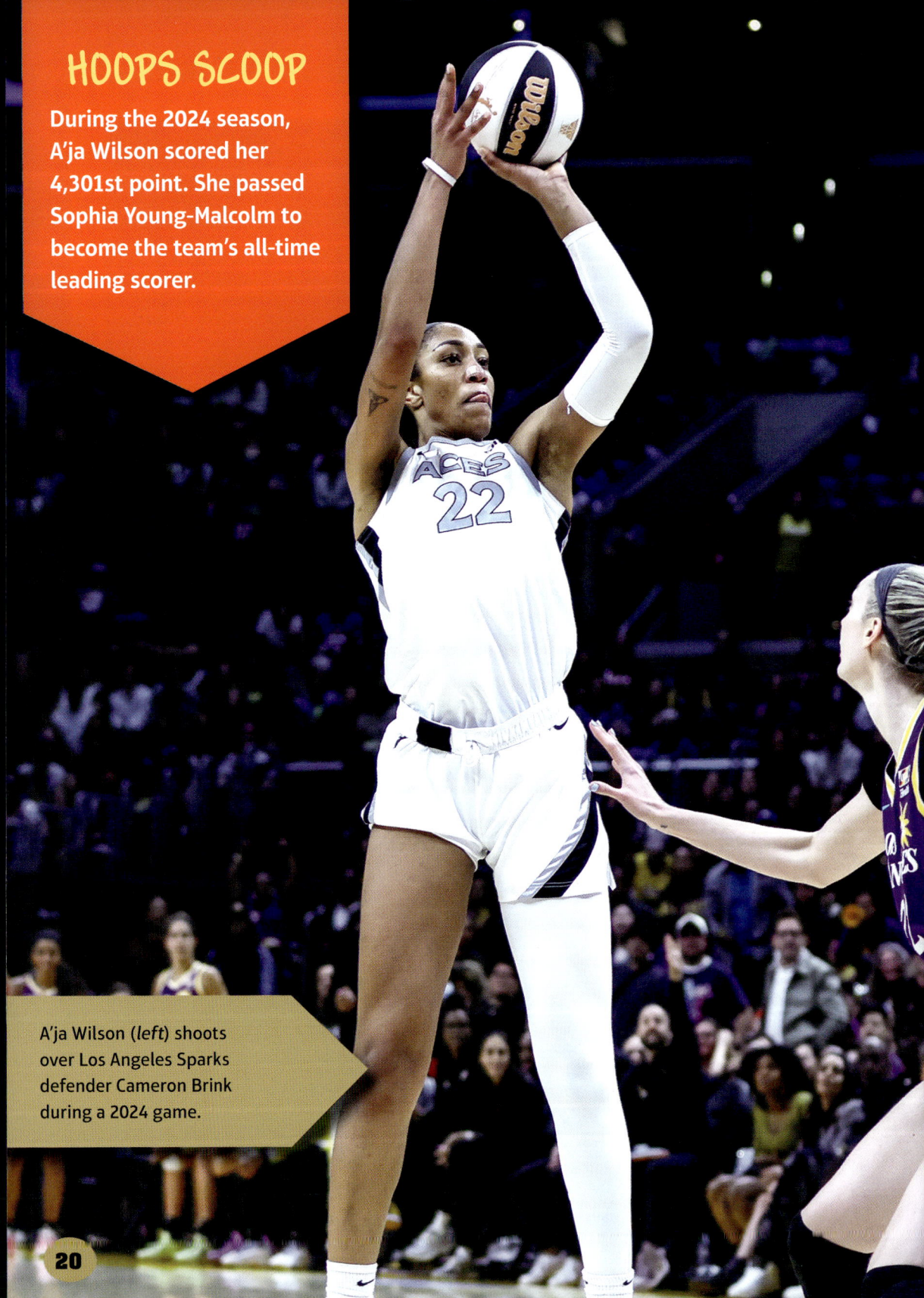

HOOPS SCOOP

During the 2024 season, A'ja Wilson scored her 4,301st point. She passed Sophia Young-Malcolm to become the team's all-time leading scorer.

A'ja Wilson (*left*) shoots over Los Angeles Sparks defender Cameron Brink during a 2024 game.

Two seasons later, Wilson won her first WNBA MVP award. In 2022, she won a second MVP award and led the Aces to their first WNBA championship. Wilson was also named the league's Defensive Player of the Year in 2022 and 2023. Her career scoring average ranks in the top five all-time.

In 2023, Wilson tied the WNBA's single-game scoring record when she scored 53 points in a game against the Atlanta Dream. In 2024, Wilson became only the fourth player in history to win the WNBA MVP three times. She shares the record with Sheryl Swoopes, Lisa Leslie, and Lauren Jackson.

Left to right: WNBA commissioner Cathy Engelbert, A'ja Wilson, and Wilson's parents at a 2022 playoff game. Wilson is holding the 2022 WNBA MVP award.

Kelsey Plum helped the Aces win two championships.

CHAPTER 3

FIRST CHAMPIONSHIP

The Aces had led Game 4 of the 2022 WNBA Finals for nearly the entire game. But the Connecticut Sun kept the game close, and they took the lead late in the fourth quarter. The Aces were looking for their first championship. A fourth-quarter collapse would be a disaster. A loss for the Aces would send the series to a deciding Game 5.

A Courtney Williams jump shot put the Sun up 69–67 with just over two minutes left in the game. Aces point guard Kelsey Plum dribbled up the court, aiming to put her team in position to score. Plum saw teammate Riquna Williams open behind the three-point line and passed her the ball. Williams dribbled and fired a three-pointer that splashed through the net, putting the Aces ahead 70–69. Moments later, a pair of free throws put the Sun back up 71–70.

Aces guard Chelsea Gray drives to the net during the 2022 WNBA Finals.

Kelsey Plum averaged 17.1 points per game during the 2022 playoffs.

Plum dribbled up the court again. She was covered by two defenders, leaving Williams open. Plum fired a pass to Williams. Williams was at the end of her career, only averaging 6.7 points per game in 2022. But Williams had once set the WNBA's single-game scoring record with 51 points in 2013.

Williams received the pass and made a three-pointer to put the Aces back up 73–71. A few seconds later, Plum spotted Williams again. This time, Williams faked a drive to the basket. She backed up and sank another jump shot to give Las Vegas a 75–71 lead. Williams had scored eight points in under 70 seconds of game time. The Aces would never trail again. They finished the game as champions with a 78–71 victory.

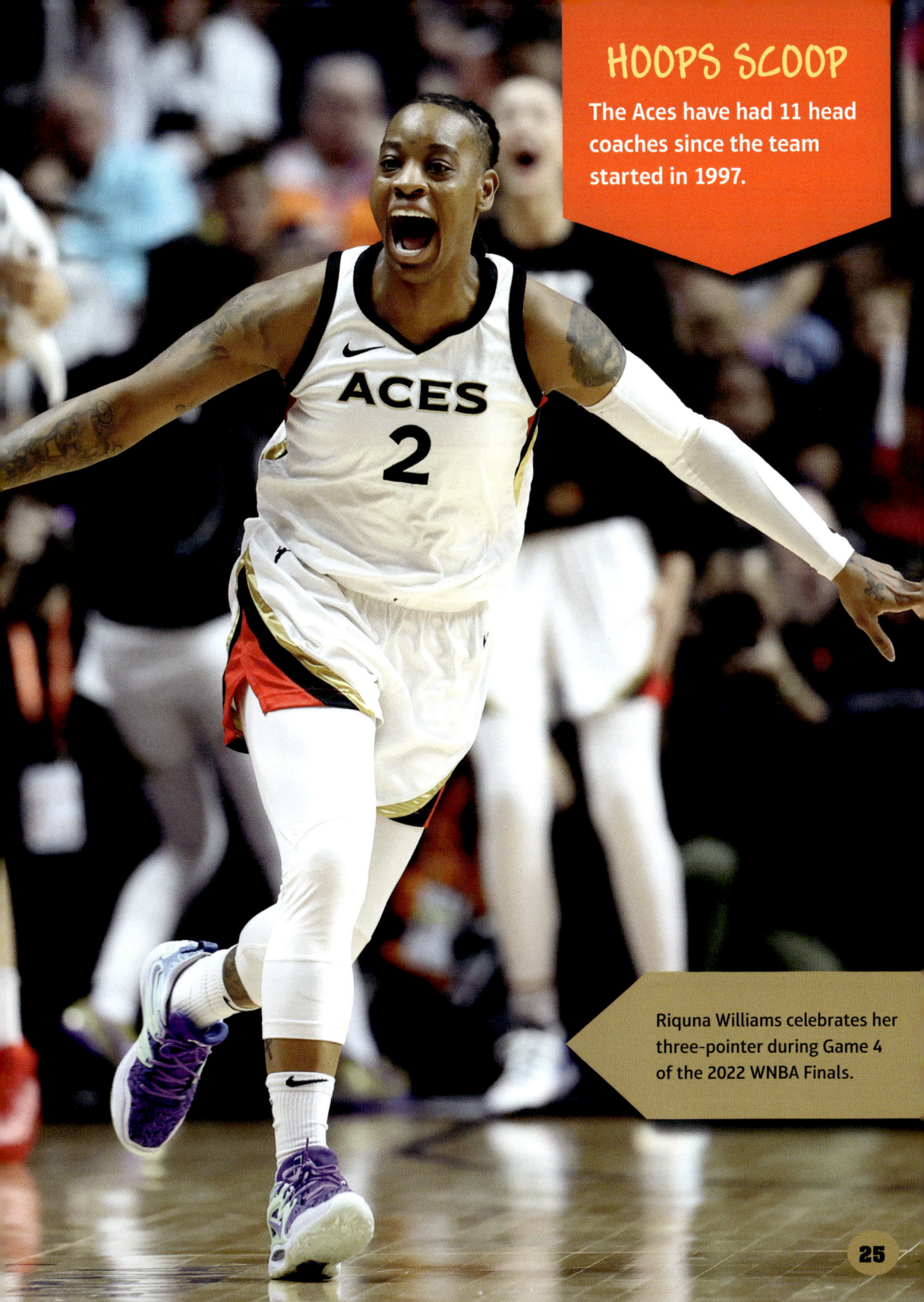

HOOPS SCOOP

The Aces have had 11 head coaches since the team started in 1997.

Riquna Williams celebrates her three-pointer during Game 4 of the 2022 WNBA Finals.

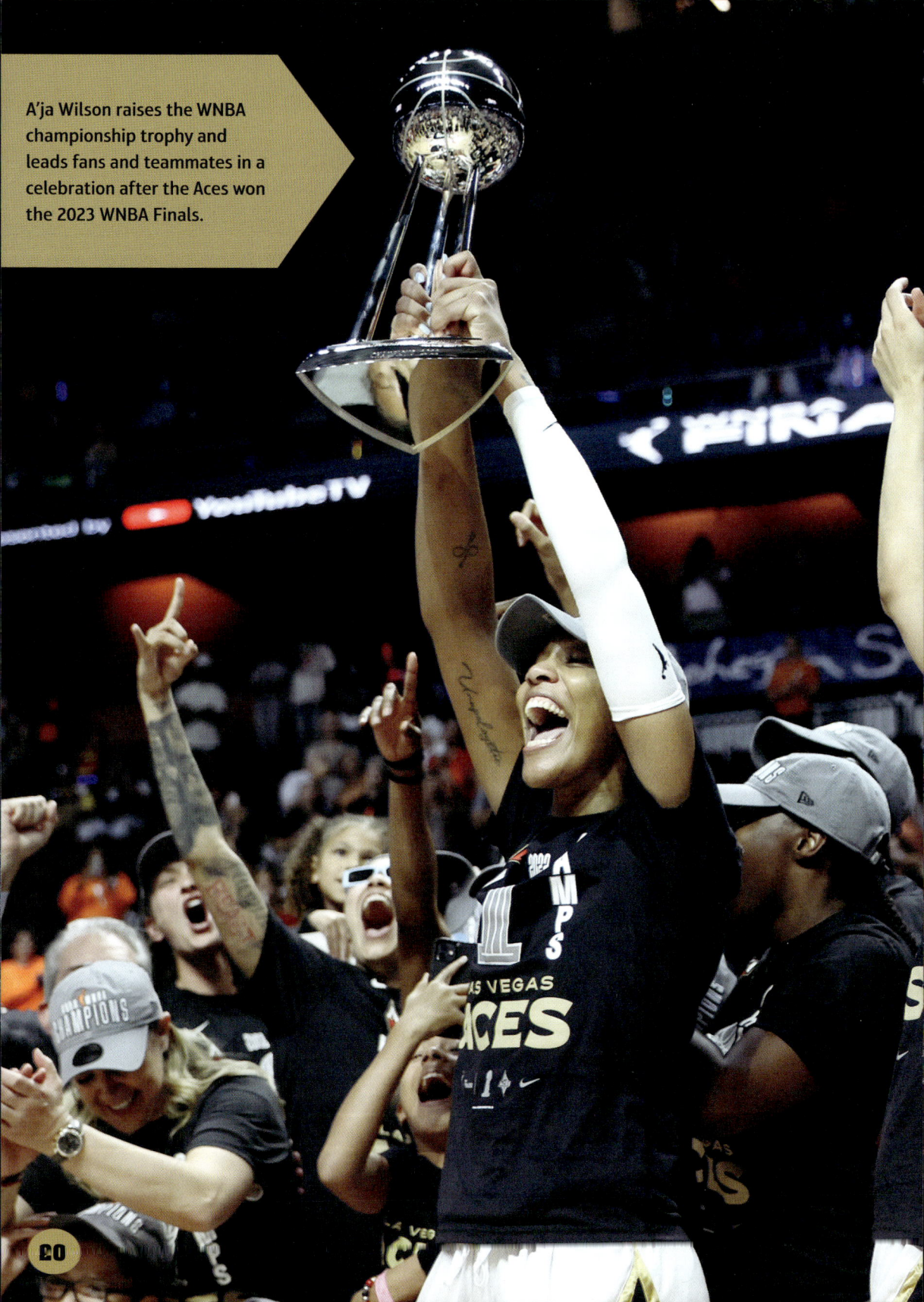

A'ja Wilson raises the WNBA championship trophy and leads fans and teammates in a celebration after the Aces won the 2023 WNBA Finals.

CHAPTER 4
A DYNASTY IN THE MAKING

The Aces are having one of the greatest periods of success by a team in league history. Las Vegas won back-to-back titles in 2022 and 2023, just after Becky Hammon was hired as coach. They were one of the league's best teams again in 2024. In addition to having the league's most dominant player in A'ja Wilson, the Aces' talent runs deep.

Jackie Young (*left*) dribbles around Dallas Wings defender Sevgi Uzun during a 2024 game.

Guard Jackie Young won the league's Most Improved Player award in 2022. She had become a steady scorer and one of the league's best three-point shooters. As a three-time All-Star, Young is often the focus of the Las Vegas offense.

Chelsea Gray has been a key player for Las Vegas since 2021. The six-time All-Star ranks eighth all-time in the WNBA with 1,631 assists. Gray was the MVP of the 2022 WNBA Finals when she averaged 18.3 points and six assists per game. She made 58 percent of her shots in the series.

After winning the league's Sixth Player of the Year award in 2021, point guard Kelsey Plum became a starter in 2022. She raised her scoring average that year by more than five points per game. She was an All-Star three seasons in a Plum was traded to the Los Angeles Sparks before the 2025 season.

Although they lost to the New York Liberty in the 2024 playoffs, the Aces have some of the WNBA's top players.

Experienced players such as Sydney Colson give the Aces an edge season after season.

The Aces finished the 2024 season second in the Western Conference with 27 wins. They made their 15th appearance in the WNBA playoffs but lost in the second round to the New York Liberty. With three-time WNBA MVP A'ja Wilson and veteran stars Chelsea Gray and Jackie Young on their roster, more fans than ever are watching the Aces play some of the league's best basketball. If another championship is in their future, the Aces may yet become a WNBA dynasty.

GLOSSARY

All-Star: a player chosen as one of the best in the league to compete in a game against other top players

assist: a pass that leads directly to a basket

Basketball Hall of Fame: a museum in Springfield, Massachusetts, that honors basketball's greatest coaches and players

dynasty: a team that is very successful for a long period of time

free throw: an open shot taken from behind a set line after a foul by an opponent

playoffs: games held after the season to determine each year's champion

rookie: a first-year player

sixth player: a key player for a team who is not usually in the starting lineup

WNBA Draft: when WNBA teams take turns choosing new players

WNBA Finals: a matchup between the two best teams in the playoffs. The winner becomes WNBA champion.

LEARN MORE

Hill, Anne E. *Inside the Las Vegas Aces*. Minneapolis: Lerner Publications, 2023.

Las Vegas Aces
https://aces.wnba.com/

Tischler, Joe. *A'ja Wilson*. Mankato, MN: Amicus Learning, 2025.

Whiting, Jim. *The Story of the Las Vegas Aces*. Mankato, MN: Creative Education and Creative Paperbacks, 2024.

WNBA
https://www.wnba.com/

Women's National Basketball Association Facts for Kids
https://kids.kiddle.co/Women%27s_National_Basketball_Association

INDEX

Clark, Alysha, 6

Connecticut Sun, 23

Dydek, Margo, 5, 10, 15

Gray, Chelsea, 28–29

Hammon, Becky, 11, 17–18, 27

Laney-Hamilton, Betnijah, 6

New York Liberty, 5, 17, 29

Plum, Kelsey, 6, 23–24, 28

Vandersloot, Courtney, 6

Williams, Courtney, 23

Williams, Riquna, 23–24

Wilson, A'ja, 5, 12, 19, 21, 27, 29

Young, Jackie, 6, 28–29

Young-Malcolm, Sophia, 11, 16–17, 20

PHOTO ACKNOWLEDGMENTS

Image credits: Sarah Stier/Getty Images, p.4; M. Anthony Nesmith/Icon Sportswire via Getty Images, p.6; Javier Vicencio/Eyepix Group/Future Publishing via Getty Images, p.7; Otto Greule Jr/Hulton Archive/Getty Images, p.8; Otto Greule Jr/Allsport/Getty Images, p. 9; Otto Greule Jr/Hulton Archive/Getty Images, p.10; Christian Petersen/Getty Images, p.11; Ethan Miller/Getty Images, p.12; Ethan Miller/Getty Images, p.13; Barry Gossage/NBAE via Getty Images/Massimo Bettiol/Getty Images, p.14; Steve Campbell/Houston Chronicle/Hearst Newspapers via Getty Images, p.15; Christian Petersen/Getty Images, p.16; TMB/Icon SMI/Icon Sportswire via Getty Images, p.17; Maddie Meyer/Getty Images, p.18; Ethan Miller/Getty Images, p.19; Jordon Kelly/Icon Sportswire via Getty Images, p.20; Ethan Miller/Getty Images, p.21; Maddie Meyer/Getty Images, p.22; Maddie Meyer/Getty Images, p.23; Maddie Meyer/Getty Images, p.24; Maddie Meyer/Getty Images, p.25; Maddie Meyer/Getty Images, p.26; Sam Hodde/Getty Images, p.27; Ethan Miller/Getty Images, p.28; Sarah Stier/Getty Images, p. 29

Cover image: Sports Press Photo/Shaina Benhiyoun/SPP/Sipa USA/Newscom